# Little Stories for Little Readers

## Levels 5-6

### Beginning Reproducible Books in English and Spanish

by:  Susan M. Ketch
     Susie Gilbert
     Joy Gornto
     Craig Johnson

Carson-Dellosa Publishing Company, Inc.
Greensboro, North Carolina

# Credits

| | |
|---|---|
| Editor: | Kelly Gunzenhauser |
| Layout Design: | Van Harris |
| Inside Illustrations: | Nathan Aaron, Joe Eckstein, Stefano Giorgi, George Ling, Wayne Miller, Bill Neville |
| Cover Design: | Peggy Jackson |
| Cover Illustrations: | Bill Neville, Dan Sharp |

ISBN 1-59441-955-8

# Table of Contents

# Introduction

Many teachers work with bright, eager students who are willing to learn and are happy to be in school but can only speak a few words of English. Many parents of English-speaking children send them to school hoping that they will have the opportunity to learn another language. There are also students from both groups who are just beginning to read or who have been trying to learn to read for a long time. And, of course, there is always that additional, unwelcome "member" of the classroom, the budget, which may limit the number of books teachers and families can purchase. *Little Stories for Little Readers* addresses all of these issues!

In this book are 12 reproducible stories that roughly correspond to most emergent readers' levels five and six. The stories are first presented in English, then retold in Spanish. Each story is illustrated with simple, black-and-white art that is perfect for coloring. Each story also has an accompanying activity page addressing different reading and language skills for native English speakers, native Spanish speakers, and children who speak other languages. To use this book, select a story, make enough copies for each student to have one, let students color the illustrations, and choose a method for students to bind the pages together. When students finish assembling the books and completing the corresponding lessons, let them take the books home to add to their personal libraries.

# Making the Books

Many reproducible books involve complicated copying, folding, and cutting. However, *Little Stories for Little Readers* pays attention to ease of use for young students and busy teachers. For each book, make single-sided copies of the pages . (For books that have the last English page and the Spanish title page on the same full-sized book page, cover the unneeded half of the page.) Have the student color each page. Then, have her cut the pages in half on the dashed lines. (Coloring before binding makes the coloring easier.) Finally, have the student turn the pages in the same direction, check that they are in the correct order, and staple them on the left side. Help students with stapling, if necessary, so that the books open easily. Students can also bind the pages using a hole punch and yarn or metal rings. As an alternative, send home bookmaking instructions and supplies so that students' families can help them make the books at home.

 Little Stories for Little Readers • CD-104200

## Special Coloring and Other Bookmaking Instructions

- Encourage students to be as creative as possible when making the books so that each book will be unique and valuable to its owner. Follow these tips to entice students to become book illustrators of the finest order. And remember, with any type of coloring other than crayon or colorful pencil, let the pages dry completely before allowing students to cut them apart.
- If desired, enlarge book pages before making class sets so that students can color them more easily.
- Students will enjoy using materials other than crayons to color their books. Let them use paint (especially watercolor), markers, glitter glue, colorful pencils, etc. Also, gear students' art media to what will work best with each book's theme. For example, while students might enjoy using blue cellophane to cover the pages with "water" in the The Ocean (page 62), they may feel that the gifts in The Party Place (page 27) would look better embellished with glitter glue and pieces of ribbon.
- Not all children's book illustrations are in color. Some students may enjoy the challenge of coloring in pencil and using different shades of gray and patterns to distinguish between areas. Provide some sample books that are illustrated in black and white, such as books by Chris Van Allsburg, before students attempt this exercise.
- Let students use torn tissue paper and watered-down glue to create collages in their books. (Students must have well-developed fine motor skills for this to work well.) This technique may require enlarging pages to big-book size.
- If your budget permits, copy the book onto different types of paper, such as pastel or brightly colored typing paper. Set aside a few blank pages on which students can try out different art techniques before applying them to the books. They will enjoy seeing how different media look on different types of paper.
- Let students be creative when binding the books. If students are careful, they can punch holes in the books and use string, yarn, ribbon, or metal rings to bind them.
- Use books for more than just reading practice. Provide tracing paper and let students trace the illustrations. This will improve their drawing abilities and fine motor skills.
- Create a class book in a unique way. Enlarge a book and then copy the pages onto transparencies. Provide write-on/wipe-away markers and let students color the pages to use on the overhead projector. Then, read the book as a class.
- Make a class set of books for students to share. Copy, cut apart, and laminate the pages. Punch holes in the pages and bind with metal rings. Store the books at a center with write-on/wipe-away markers. Allow students to visit the center to color the books. Provide paper towels so that each student may erase the previous student's work before coloring a book.

## Using the Books with Students

In addition to supplementing the classroom library, these books can serve a variety of purposes. Students can make and take home up to 24 different books if both the English and Spanish versions are used, which can significantly increase some students' personal libraries. Spanish speakers will feel good about reading books on the same level as their English-speaking classmates. Students who speak primarily English or Spanish can broaden their vocabularies and increase their fluency. And, best of all, students will have access to more quality stories. Use the following activities to incorporate the little stories into the classroom.

- Teach new concepts and vocabulary with the little stories. Before sharing the stories with the class, preview them and note any concepts or words you feel may be challenging for students. Then, plan activities to complete prior to the reading that will help students be familiar with new words or concepts. For example, before reading the story The Ocean (pages 62–71), teach the word *coral* by showing pictures or bringing in a sample. To introduce the story The Builder (pages 45–54), provide a tape measure for students to use to measure classroom objects. Look for these and additional suggestions for introducing new words and concepts in the activity page before each story.

- Help a new Spanish-speaking student feel welcome in an English-speaking classroom by making him a guest reader. Let the student choose one of the stories to share with the class. Have the class color, cut out, and bind both versions of the story. Allow the guest reader to practice reading the story to you or a partner until he feels comfortable. Then, read the English version aloud to the class and let the student read the Spanish version. Explain that his reading is meant to be an example of how native Spanish speakers sound. Then, let other students meet in small groups to chorally read the story in Spanish, following the example of the native speaker.

- Use the books to teach the English and Spanish alphabet. Assign a story that has several letters in common between the two versions. Have each student color, cut apart, and assemble both versions of the book. Then, have students go on a scavenger hunt for the assigned letters and use colorful pencils to circle the letters as they find them. Write some of the words on the board and talk about the different sounds the letters make in both languages. Be sure to point out the letters that appear in only the Spanish alphabet (ch, ll, ñ, rr) where appropriate. (Note that some Spanish speakers no longer include some of these as separate letters in their alphabet.)

- Use a story to teach new words. Give the Spanish version to English speakers and vice versa. Provide a copy of the glossary (pages 124–128) for each student. Let students underline unfamiliar words in colorful pencil and look up those words in the glossary. Then, students should color and cut apart the pages. Have students create mini-dictionaries for their books on the blank backs of the last pages of their books. Set aside time for students to study and learn the new words. Then, let each student bring her book to your desk. Read the story with her and ask her what each underlined word means.

- Have a "magic word" reading. For this activity, provide English books for native Spanish speakers and Spanish books for English speakers. Explain that you will read the story in students' nonnative language. Then, choose an important word from the story, talk about it in the native language, and have students try to guess which nonnative word corresponds to the native word as you read. For example, in the story My Best Buddy (pages 36–44), choose a word like *buddy* (amigo) and see if students can guess which word it might be as you read the story in Spanish.

- Practice fluency in any language. Enlarge a story or copy it onto a transparency. Share it aloud with the class in both languages. Then, let students make their own copies of the mini-book. Assign half of the class to read in English and the other half to read in Spanish. Have a class read-aloud time. As you show the pages in your copy, let students chorally read along in their assigned languages, taking turns for every page. Then, let pairs of students continue practicing together in the same way. When students are fluent in their assigned languages, have them swap books. Repeat the class choral reading and the pair practice until students are fluently reading the story in both languages.

- Partner reading in two languages can be fun. Pair a fluent English reader with a fluent Spanish reader. Have the partners agree on one story they would both like to turn into a book. Let the Spanish reader color the English book and vice versa. Then, instruct students to swap books and read aloud to each other. Tell students to pay attention to how their partners are reading because they will be reading in their nonnative languages next. When students have heard the stories read aloud, let them swap books and read aloud again. Have the English reader coach the Spanish reader on her English pronunciation and reading and let the Spanish reader coach the English reader on his Spanish pronunciation. Finally, let both students read their story aloud to the class. Compliment each pair on some aspect of their effort, such as teamwork, pronunciation, fluency, or expression.

- Students benefit from hearing their reading improve. Use a tape recorder as students practice reading the stories in either language. Have a student record herself reading a story for the first time. Let her practice it four times. Then, record the reading a second time. After the second recording, let the student listen to both of her readings to demonstrate that practice does make perfect.

- Let Spanish- and English-speaking students use their native languages to improve their expression when reading in nonnative languages. Allow each student to practice reading a story fluently in his native language (English or Spanish) and then record himself. Work with the student on his expression while reading. Then, have him play back the recording and talk with him about positive aspects of his reading. Next, let the student record himself reading the story in his nonnative language, attempting to recreate the same expression and fluency he used in the first, native reading. Compare the two readings and make additional assignments according to the student's individual needs.

- Choose a different pair of stories for students to use to make books each week. After the books are made, select vocabulary from the stories and have a bilingual spelling bee. Assign students a list of Spanish and English words from the story. Refer them to the glossary (page 124–128) for definitions. Then, have a spelling bee. Divide the class into two teams. Try to assign an equal number of native English and Spanish speakers to each team. Call out the words randomly in either English or Spanish. For example, for the story My Best Buddy (pages 36–44), give the first student in line for Team A the word *amigo* (friend or buddy) to spell, define, give the English equivalent of, etc. If the student is correct, give that team a point. If the student is incorrect, allow Team B a turn to spell, define, or give the English equivalent for a point. Alternate between Spanish and English words for both teams. The team with the most points at the end of the game wins. As a reward, let the winning team choose the story for the next spelling bee.

# That Made Me Mad!

Craig Johnson  Level 5

Number of English Words: 51
Number of Spanish Words: 51

## Pre-Reading Activities

*Book Introduction:* The name of this story is *That Made Me Mad!* Things happen at school that make a boy mad. A hug from a friend makes him glad.

*Discussion Suggestions:* Ask, "Would the things that made this boy mad make you mad? Is it okay to get mad? What made the boy feel better?"

*Word Work:*
Structure—Point out that *That made me mad!* is a pattern, as is *¡Eso me hizo enojar!*
Sight words—Students should learn to read *I, my, that,* and *me.*
Rhyming words—*mad/glad, -ed* chunk
Punctuation—Identify exclamation points.

## Post-Reading Questions/Activities

1. What makes you mad? Why?
2. Have any of the things that happened to the boy in the story happened to you?
3. What do you do when you get mad?

## Extension Activities

1. Have students write and illustrate stories to answer the above questions. Staple the pages to make books.
2. Have students make lists of emotions, cut them apart, then sort them according to whether the emotion feels good or bad.
3. Talk about the fact that different things make people mad. Brainstorm things students can do when they are mad, such as count to 10, talk things out, etc.

## Related Literature

- *Alexander and the Terrible, Horrible, No Good, Very Bad Day* by Judith Viorst (Atheneum, 1972)
- *The Giant's Boy* by Joy Cowley (Wright Group, 1987)
- *How Do I Feel?* by Norma Simon (Albert Whitman & Company, 1977)
- *I Was So Mad!* by Norma Simon (Albert Whitman & Company, 1991)
- *Mr. Grump* by Joy Cowley (Wright Group, 1993)

## Translation Notes

The Spanish word for *I* is *yo.* In the Spanish language, as in English, the verb endings can change according to the pronoun used and can also change according to the verb tense. The difference is that in Spanish, the change includes the pronoun as well as the word. For example, the word *romper* means *to break. Rompí* means *I broke.* Many Spanish language learners might say, *"Yo rompí el lápiz."* While not exactly incorrect, the form can be redundant. The speaker would literally be saying, *"I I broke the pencil."* However, including the pronoun works well when the speaker wants to emphasize the identity of the subject.

Little Stories for Little Readers • CD-104200

# That Made Me Mad!

Written by Craig Johnson

Illustrated by Bill Neville

I missed my bus. That made me mad!

**I spilled my milk. That made me mad!**

**I dropped my books. That made me mad!**

# I broke my pencil. That made me mad!

# I fell on the playground. That made me mad!

My friend gave me a hug. That made me glad!

¡Eso me hizo enojar!

Escrito por Craig Johnson          Ilustrado por Bill Neville

**Perdí el autobús. ¡Eso me hizo enojar!**

**Tiré mi leche. ¡Eso me hizo enojar!**

## Se me cayeron los libros. ¡Eso me hizo enojar!

## Rompí mi lápiz. ¡Eso me hizo enojar!

# Me caí en el patio de recreo. ¡Eso me hizo enojar!

# Mi amigo me dio un abrazo. ¡Eso me puso contento!

# Bubble Gum

Susie Gilbert

## Level 5

Number of English Words: 81
Number of Spanish Words: 74

## Pre-Reading Activities

**Book Introduction:** The name of this book is *Bubble Gum*. The girl in the story likes bubble gum. She can blow bubbles in many shapes and sizes.

**Discussion Suggestions:** Ask, "Do you chew bubble gum? Can you blow a bubble? What kinds of bubbles would you like to blow?"

**Picture Walk:**
Theme—Ask, "Do you think anyone could blow a bubble as big as a house?" Explain that the girl exaggerates about the kinds of bubbles she can blow.
Structure—Point out and compare shapes and sizes of bubbles.

**Word Work:**
Introduce the concept of the phrase *as big as I wish* (page 2) by first talking about wishes. Then, explain that the word *wish* is used like the word *want* in this instance.
Rhyming words—*fish/wish, mouse/house, sky/fly, day/play* (Note that in Spanish, these words do not rhyme.)
Sight words—Students should learn to read *can, big, look,* and *like*. Word endings—Note inflectional endings *-s* and *-ing*.

## Post-Reading Activities

1. Ask, "How do you know that the girl likes bubble gum? How do you know that the girl is exaggerating about the kinds of bubbles she can blow?"
2. Have students look at the last page and guess why the bubble might have popped.

## Extension Activities

1. Let students draw pictures of bubbles they would like to blow. Have them outline the shapes with pink glue (white glue tinted with red food coloring). Allow them to dry.
2. Survey students in your classroom to see who can blow a bubble, what are favorite gum flavors, etc. Graph the results.

## Related Literature

- *Bubble Gum, Bubble Gum* by Lisa Wheeler (Megan Tingley, 2004)
- *The Gum on the Drum* by Barbara Gregorich (School Zone, 1992)

## Translation Notes

In this translation, the word *hacer* is used for *to blow. Hacer* actually means *to do* or *to make*. Show students that the last word in the story, *Pop,* is the same in both languages. Then, point out that in Spanish an interjection or exclamatory word or sentence has an exclamation point both before (upside down) and after the word or sentence, as in the word *¡Pop!*

Little Stories for Little Readers • CD-104200

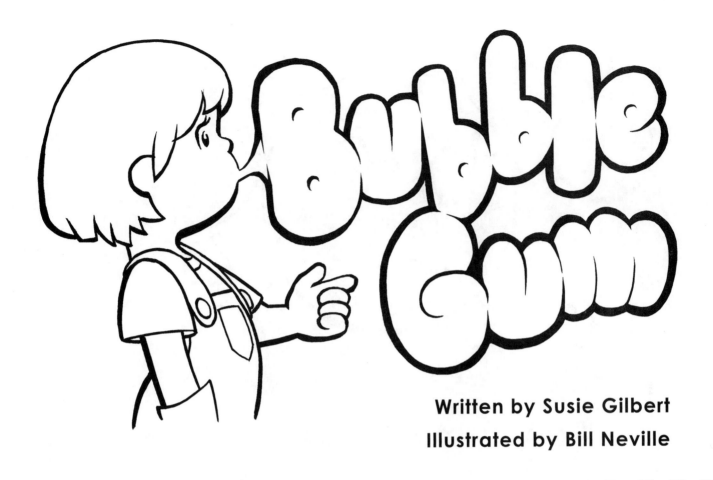

Written by Susie Gilbert

Illustrated by Bill Neville

I can blow a bubble that looks like a fish.

I can blow a bubble as big as I wish.

Now, my bubble looks like a mouse.

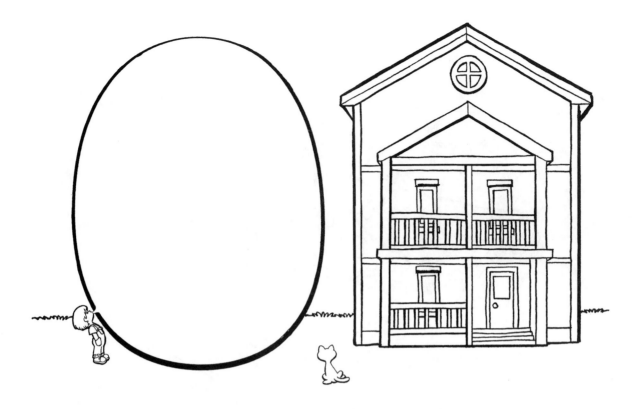

## My bubble is growing as big as a house.

Bubble Gum • CD-104200 • © Carson-Dellosa

## I can blow a bubble as big as the sky.

Bubble Gum • CD-104200 • © Carson-Dellosa

## My bubble can even make me fly.

## I like to blow bubbles. I can blow them all day.

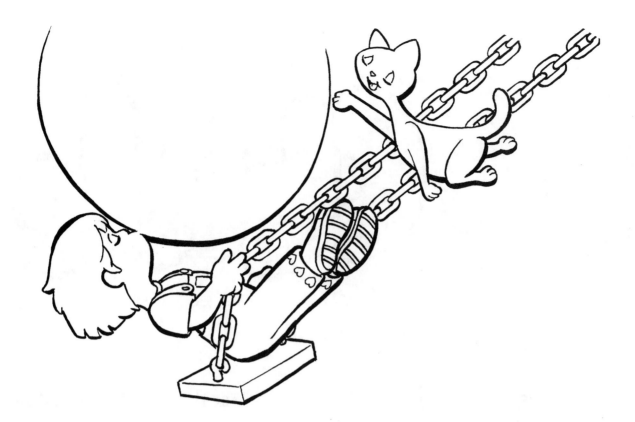

I blow bubbles as I swing when I go out to play.

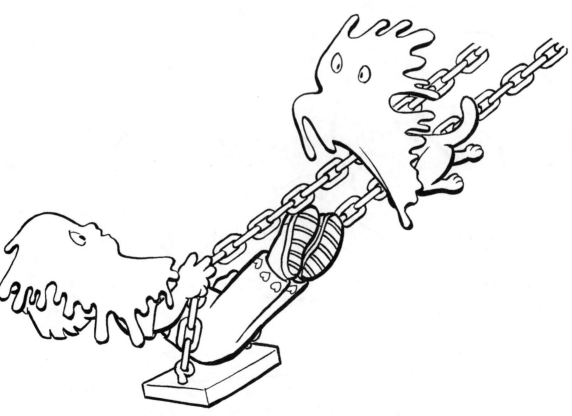

I like bubble gum. POP!

# Chicle

**Escrito por Susie Gilbert**

**Ilustrado por Bill Neville**

**Puedo hacer un globo que parece un pez.**

**Puedo hacer un globo tan grande como quiero.**

**Ahora mi globo parece un ratón.**

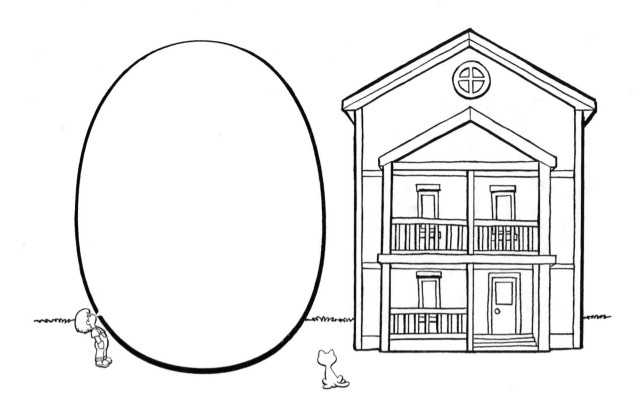

**Ahora mi globo está creciendo tan grande como una casa.**

- - - - - - - - - - - - - - - - - - - - - - - - - - - - - - - - - - - -

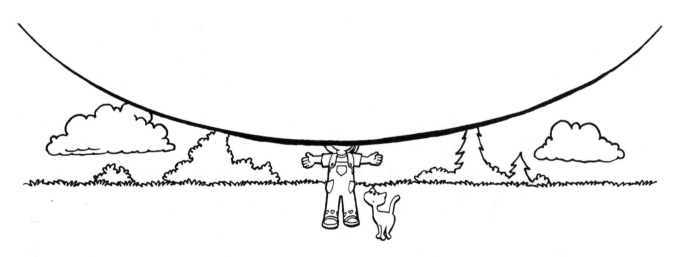

**Puedo hacer un globo tan grande como el cielo.**

**Ahora mi globo hasta me hace volar.**

**Me gusta hacer globos. Puedo hacer globos todo el día.**

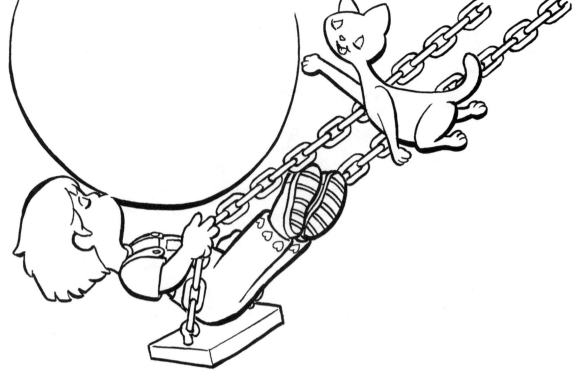

**Cuando salgo a jugar puedo hacer un globo mientras me columpio.**

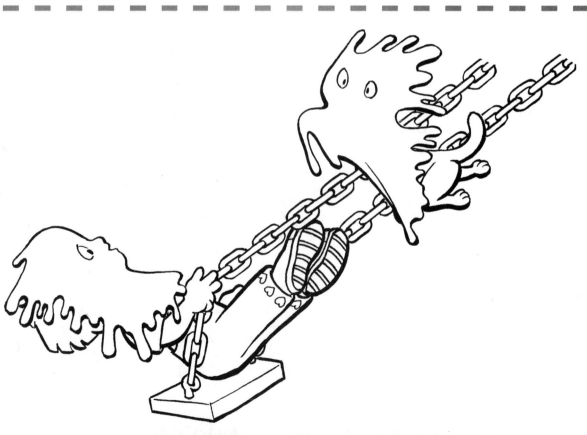

**Me gusta el chicle. ¡POP!**

# The Party Place

Susan M. Ketch    Level 5

Number of English Words: 50
Number of Spanish Words: 46

## Pre-Reading Activities

*Book Introduction:* The name of this book is *The Party Place.* It is about a place for having birthday parties, holiday parties, and just-for-fun parties.

*Discussion Suggestions:* Say, "Think about a party you have been to. What decorations did you see? Did you wear special clothes or hats? Were there presents? Did you have fun?"

*Picture Walk:* Point out the children's happy faces and what they are doing. Also, explain what balloon animals are and ask who has seen any. Talk about the treat bags on page 6.

*Word Work:*
Punctuation—Point out exclamation points, the comma, and the ellipses. Also, note the two exclamation points used in the Spanish version of the story.
Sight words—Students should learn to sight read the words *come, we, have,* and *us.*
Word analogies—Compare the words *at/hat.*
Structure—Point out that *We have _____* is a recurring pattern, as is *Tenemos.*

## Post-Reading Activities

1. Have students name some of the things this party had. What kind of party is going on in this book?
2. Let a few students tell about the most recent parties they attended.

## Extension Activities

1. Let each student pretend she is having a party and create invitations.
2. Parties require many supplies. Let each student make a list of the things he would need for the party.
3. Have each student draw a picture of what her party will look like, showing decorations and happy faces.

## Related Literature

- *The Cake That Mack Ate* by Rose Robart (Megan Tingley, 1991)
- *Miss Spider's Tea Party* by David Kirk (Scholastic, 1994)
- *Spot's Birthday Party* by Eric Hill (Puffin, 2003)

## Translation Notes

To many native English speakers in North America, the word *sombrero* represents a traditional-style hat with a wide brim and a pointed top. However, *sombrero* is also the Spanish word for any kind of hat.

Point out the words *¡Yum! ¡Yum! ¡Yum!* Sometimes, Spanish words are really just English words that have become common in Spanish. And, many common English words are actually Spanish words, like *taco, armadillo,* and *pronto,* which means *at once.*

# THE PARTY PLACE

Written by Susan M. Ketch    Illustrated by Joe Eckstein

## Come inside, and you will see . . .

. . . the party place!

We have funny hats. Look at us!

**We have balloons. They are red, green, blue, and yellow.**

**We have cake, cookies, and juice to drink. Yum! Yum! Yum!**

# We have presents, lots of presents!

# We have fun at the party place!

# EL LUGAR DE LA FIESTA

**Escrito por Susan M. Ketch    Ilustrado por Joe Eckstein**

**Ven adentro y verás . . .**

. . . ¡el lugar de la fiesta!

Es Mi Cumpleaños

## Tenemos sombreros cómicos. ¡Míranos!

**Tenemos globos. Son rojos, verdes, azules y amarillos.**

**Tenemos una tarta, unas galletas y jugo para beber. ¡Yum! ¡Yum! ¡Yum!**

¡Tenemos regalos, muchos regalos!

¡Nos divertimos mucho en el lugar de la fiesta!

# My Best Buddy

Craig Johnson    Level 5

Number of English Words: 67
Number of Spanish Words: 66

## Pre-Reading Activities

*Book Introduction:* The name of this book is *My Best Buddy*. A dad tells his son that the son is good at doing many things.

*Discussion Suggestions:* Ask, "What do your family members think you are good at doing? What do they like best about you?"

*Picture Walk:* Name each task that the boy is doing throughout the book.

*Word Work:*
Sight words—Students should learn to sight read *my, dad, me, you, are, he, I, like,* and *do.*
Structure—Point out that *My dad tells me* and *You are good at* are recurring patterns. *Mi papá me dice* also repeats.
Type treatment—Ask students why they think that *everything* and *todo* are underlined.

## Post-Reading Activities

1. Have students write and illustrate stories about their dads or other family members who like the way they do things.
2. Let students brainstorm a list of things that they are good at doing.

## Extension Activities

1. Explain that everyone can do something special. Ask students to think about skills that they could easily teach to others, such as wiggling ears, blowing a big bubble, etc. Ask each student to show his special talent to two other people.

## Related Literature

- *The Daddy Book* by Todd Parr (Megan Tingley, 2002)
- *The Giant's Boy* by Joy Cowley (Wright Group, 1987)
- *When Dad Went to Daycare* by Joy Cowley (Wright Group, 1987)

## Translation Notes

Note the difference between *Tú eres bueno en lectura* and *Tú juegas bien a la pelota conmigo. You are good at* is an idiom. Idioms are difficult to translate. In English, *You are good at* can be used with most *-ing* words. In Spanish, the verb makes a difference. Therefore, the first sentence means *You are good at reading,* while the second one says *You play ball well with me.*

In the Spanish version, the pronouns *tú* on pages 1–5 and *yo* on page 6 are not entirely necessary because the verb forms change according to the pronouns. However, to help both English- and Spanish-speaking readers recognize these important words in the other language, as well as the recurring pattern, the pronouns have been included.

# My Best Buddy

Written by Craig Johnson

Illustrated by Bill Neville

My dad tells me, "You are my best buddy."

**He tells me, "You are good at reading."**

**My dad tells me, "You are good at drawing."**

**My dad tells me, "You are good at playing ball with me."**

**He tells me, "You are good at hugging me."**

**I tell my dad, "You like <u>everything</u> I do!"**

**He tells me, "Yes, I do. You are my best buddy."**

# Mi mejor amigo

**Escrito por Craig Johnson**

**Ilustrado por Bill Neville**

**Mi papá me dice, "Tú eres mi mejor amigo".**

**Él me dice, "Tú eres bueno en lectura".**

Mi mejor amigo • CD-104200 • © Carson-Dellosa

**Mi papá me dice, "Tú dibujas bien".**

Mi mejor amigo • CD-104200 • © Carson-Dellosa

**Mi papá me dice, "Tú juegas bien a la pelota conmigo".**

**Él me dice, "Tú me abrazas bien".**

**Yo le digo a mi papá, ¡"A ti te gusta <u>todo</u> lo que yo hago"!**

**Él me dice, "Sí. Tú eres mi mejor amigo".**

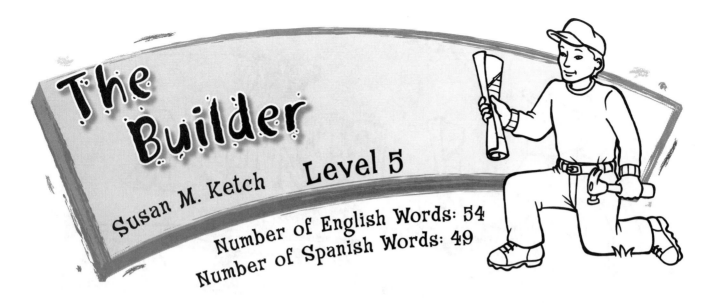

# The Builder

Susan M. Ketch   Level 5

Number of English Words: 54
Number of Spanish Words: 49

## Pre-Reading Activities

*Book Introduction:* The name of this book is *The Builder*. The man in the story is a builder. He uses many tools to build a house.

*Discussion Suggestions:* Ask, "Have you seen a house being built? Does someone in your family build things? What tools does he use? Do you help?" Provide a tape measure for students to use to measure classroom objects.

*Picture Walk:* Point out the frame of the house and note that the builder must use many different tools when he builds. Have students identify the tools on each page. Also, help students read the "wooden" title.

*Word Work:*
Sight words—Students should learn to sight read *the* and *will*.
Word analogies—Compare the sounds of the words *will/drill*. Note the *-s* chunk in *tools*, *screws*, and *holes*.
Structure—Point out that *The _____ will* is a recurring pattern.
Vocabulary—Familiarize students with the term *tape measure*. Show how one is used.

## Post-Reading Activities

1. Ask students to name the tools the builder uses. Have them brainstorm other tools.
2. Let students name other people who use tools to do their jobs, such as teachers, stylists, plumbers, etc.
3. Talk about the surprise at the end—that the builder has built a treehouse.

## Extension Activities

1. Using blocks, action figures, and paper scraps, let students build structures and then explain what they have built.
2. Note that builders use plans called *blueprints*. Let students draw blueprints for a new building.
3. Provide "safe" tools for students to try out, such as wrenches, levels, tape measures, etc. Make sure students are closely supervised. Or, purchase a set of inexpensive, plastic tools.

## Related Literature

- *Building a House* by Byron Barton (HarperTrophy, 1990)
- *Fix-It* by David McPhail (Puffin, 1992)
- *The Toolbox* by Anne Rockwell (Walker, 2004)

## Translation Notes

Explain that *el, la, los,* and *las* all mean "the." But, these words change gender and number along with the nouns they precede. Some of the tool names are preceded by *la* because these are singular nouns with the feminine ending (*-a*), while others are preceded by *el* because they have a masculine ending (usually *-o*). Also, *él* with an accent mark means *he*.

# THE BUILDER

Written by Susan M. Ketch    Illustrated by George Ling

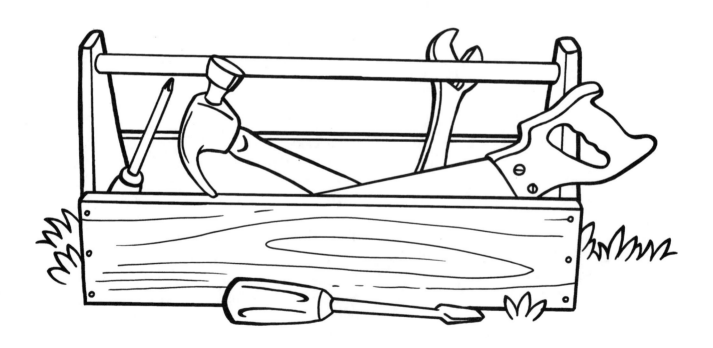

The builder has many tools.

# He uses the tools to build a house.

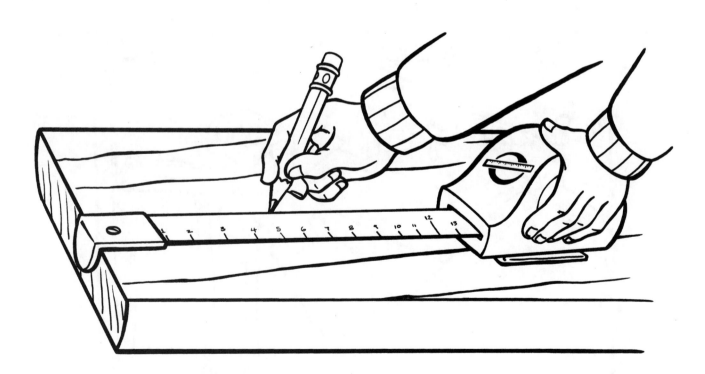

# The tape measure will measure the wood.

## The saw will cut the wood.

## The hammer will hit the nail.

## The drill will make the holes.

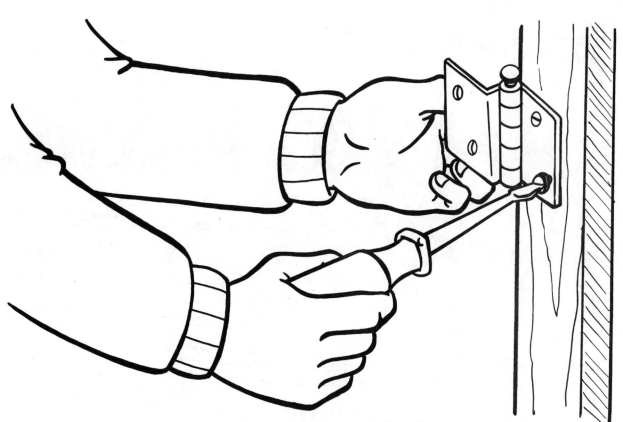

## The screwdriver will put in the screws.

The builder uses many tools to build a house.

# EL CONSTRUCTOR

**Escrito por Susan M. Ketch**      **Ilustrado por George Ling**

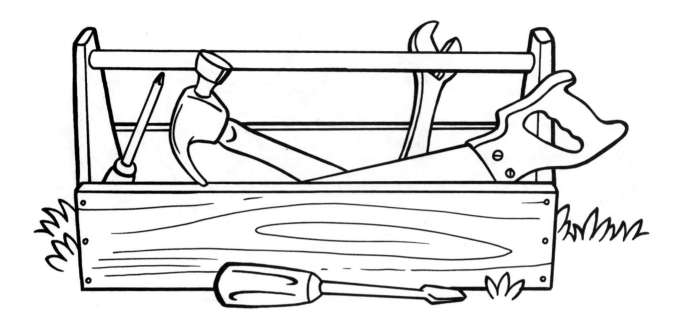

# El constructor tiene muchas herramientas.

# Él usa las herramientas para construir una casa.

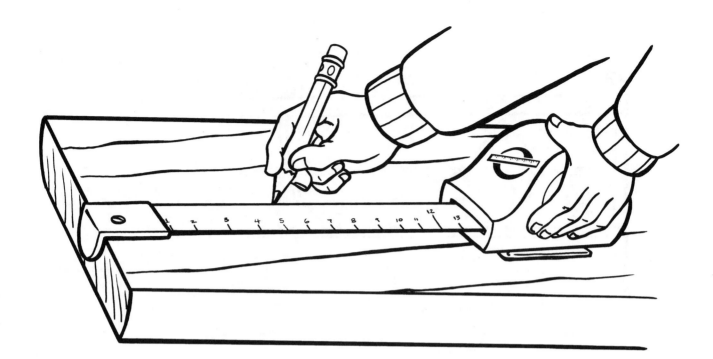

## La cinta de medir medirá la madera.

## La sierra cortará la madera.

**El martillo le pegará al clavo.**

**El taladro hará agujeros.**

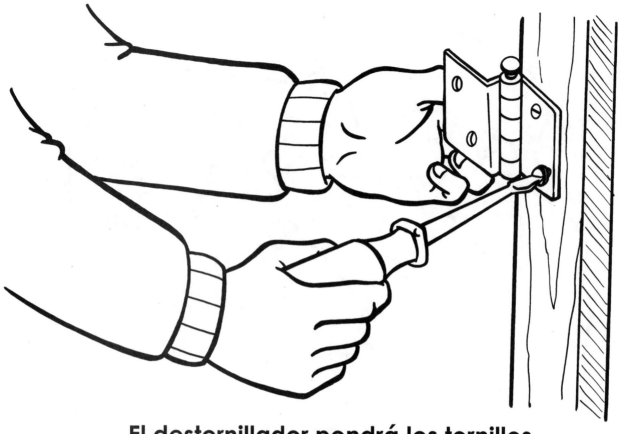

**El destornillador pondrá los tornillos.**

**El constructor usa muchas herramientas para construir una casa.**

# As Big . . .

Susan M. Ketch    Level 5

Number of English Words: 39
Number of Spanish Words: 39

## Pre-Reading Activities

*Book Introduction:* The name of this book is *As Big . . . .* A boy finds things in his house that are as big as he is.

*Discussion Suggestions:* Ask, "Do you know how tall you are? How much have you grown since you were a baby? Are all children the same size at the same age?"

*Picture Walk:* Name each task the boy does.

*Word Work:*
Sight words—Students should learn to sight read *my, as,* and *is.*
Word analogies—Compare *as* and *is.*
Structure—Point out that *My* ____ *is/are as big as* ____ is a repeating pattern, as is *tan grande/s como* ____.

## Post-Reading Activities

1. Ask, "What did the boy compare his feet to?"
2. Find out if students know any twins. Discuss the fact that identical twins look exactly alike, but fraternal twins can look different and even be a boy and a girl.
3. Tell each student to think of something that is the same size as he is.

## Extension Activities

1. As a class, list measuring tools, such as measuring cups, spoons, rulers, etc.

2. With magnetic letters, make the word *is.* Then, put the letter *h* in front of the word *is.* Ask students what word you have made. Repeat with the word *as.*
3. Let each student write a story about a set of identical twins. Discuss what could be good about being a twin and what might be difficult.

## Related Literature

- *Just Like Everyone Else* by Karla Kuskin (HarperCollins, 1982)
- *Meg and Mog* by Helen Nicoll (Viking, 1976)
- *You'll Soon Grow into Them, Titch* by Pat Hutchins (HarperTrophy, 1992)

## Translation Notes

Explain that *mi* and *mis* both mean *my.* The first is singular and the second is plural in order to match words they describe, like *libros* in the phrase *mis libros.* In Spanish, singular nouns have singular possessive pronouns, and plural nouns have plural possessive pronouns. (These are also called possessive adjectives.)

The Spanish word for *puzzle* is *rompecabezas.* It takes its name from its action: *romper* (*to break*) and its object: *cabeza* (*head*). This is similar in English to a *head-scratcher* or *brainteaser.* Other Spanish words formed in this manner include *lavaplatos* (*dishwasher*) and *rascacielos* (*skyscraper*).

As
BIG...

Written by Susan M. Ketch
Illustrated by Nathan Aaron

## My head is as big as a plate.

## My body is as big as a pillow.

## My hands are as big as a book.

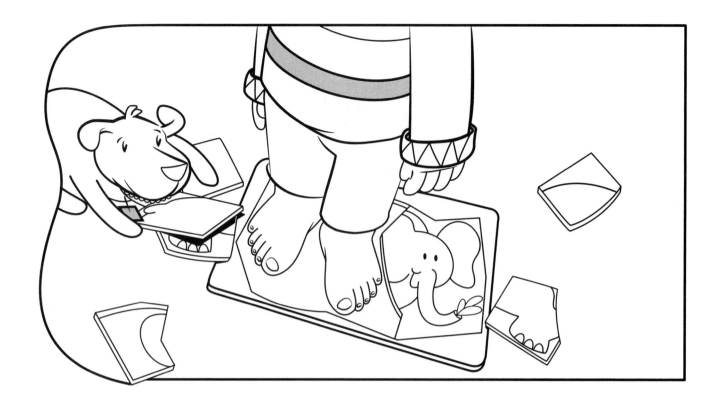

## My feet are as big as a puzzle.

## I am as big as my brother.

TAN GRANDE COMO...

Escrito por Susan M. Ketch
Ilustrado por Nathan Aaron

## Mi cabeza es tan grande como un plato.

**Mi cuerpo es tan grande como una almohada.**

**Mis manos son tan grandes como un libro.**

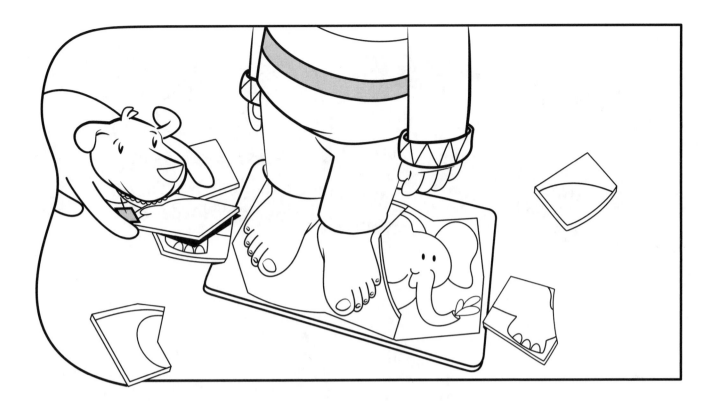

# Mis pies son tan grandes como un rompecabezas.

# Yo soy tan grande como mi hermano.

# The Ocean

Susan M. Ketch    Level 6

Number of English Words: 89
Number of Spanish Words: 83

## Pre-Reading Activities

*Book Introduction:* The name of this book is *The Ocean*. The ocean is a large body of water. It is home to many fish and plants.

*Discussion Suggestions:* Ask, "Have you ever seen an ocean? Use describing words to tell about it. Did you notice the waves? Some days the ocean is rough, and some days it is calm."

*Picture Walk:* Have students describe each picture. Point out the different sizes of fish.

*Word Work:*
Sight words—Students should learn to sight read color words as well as *has* and *little*.
Word analogies—Compare the sounds of the words *some/come* and *hide/side/ride* and the sounds and meanings of *big/bigger*.
Vocabulary—If possible, bring in pictures or a sample of *coral*. Explain that fish and tiny plants (algae) use coral for food and shelter.

## Post-Reading Activities

1. Have students talk about ocean sounds using descriptive words. Then, repeat with ocean smells.
2. Talk about what it would be like to live in the ocean. Let students describe what kinds of houses they might live in.

## Extension Activities

1. Let students research to find out how large a gray whale may grow (about 45 feet or 14 meters). Measure along the floor or wall and mark the length of a whale. Then, see how many children can line up along the length.
2. Draw, color, and cut out fish. Glue them to a long piece of blue paper. Attach plastic ocean plants and real shells to create a mural.
3. Have students write about what kinds of fish they would like to be and why.

## Related Literature

- *Beach Day* by Helen Oxenbury (Dial, 1982)
- *Morning Beach* by Leslie A. Baker (Little, Brown & Co., 1990)
- *What's Under the Ocean* by Janet Craig (Troll, 1996)

## Translation Notes

Point out the accent mark in *océano*. One reason there are accents in Spanish has to do with pronunciation. Just like in English, most pronunciations follow a pattern—a way certain combinations of letters are typically pronounced. But, also like in English, there are exceptions. In a typical four-syllable Spanish word, such as *amarillo*, the emphasis is on the third syllable. In *océano*, the emphasis is on the second syllable. The accent mark shows where to put that emphasis.

While some Spanish speakers use *cuerpo de agua*, others may be familiar with *masa de agua*, which literally means *mass of water*.

# The Ocean

Written by Susan M. Ketch
Illustrated by Wayne Miller

## The ocean is a big body of water.

**The ocean has waves that come in and go out.**

**The ocean is full of plants, coral, and fish.**

**The large fish wants to eat the little fish.**

**The small fish hide in the coral to keep away from the bigger fish.**

**The ocean has a beach of sand, rocks, and shells.**

**It is fun to dig in the sand and build a sand castle.**

The ocean is home to many plants and fish. It is a fun place to play.

# El océano

**Escrito por Susan M. Ketch**
**Ilustrado por Wayne Miller**

**El océano es un gran cuerpo de agua.**

**El océano tiene olas que vienen y van.**

**El océano está lleno de plantas, corales y peces.**

**El pez grande quiere comerse a los peces pequeños.**

**Los peces chicos se esconden en los corales para alejarse de los peces enormes.**

**El océano tiene un playa de arena, rocas y conchas.**

**Es divertido excavar en la arena y hacer castillos de arena.**

**El océano aloja a muchas plantas y peces. Es un lugar divertido para jugar.**

# Can I Go, Too?

Susan M. Ketch    Level 6

Number of English Words: 85
Number of Spanish Words: 84

## Pre-Reading Activities

*Book Introduction:* The name of this book is *Can I Go, Too?*. This girl has a busy family. She asks to go to work with each of them.

*Discussion Suggestions:* Ask, "Who works in your family? Where do they work? Have you ever gone to work with someone? Do you have a job at school or around the house?"

*Picture Walk:* As students look through the book, see if they can guess where each person works by looking at his clothes and/or the workplace. Ask if they have been to any of the places shown in the pictures.

*Word Work:*
Punctuation—Identify quotation marks and question marks.
Word analogies—Compare the endings of the words *go/goes* and *to/too*. Also, compare the pronouns *his* and *her*.
Structure—Point out that *My ____ goes ____* and *Can I go, too, ____?* are recurring patterns, as are *va a su trabajo* and *¿Puedo ir yo también, ____?*
Contractions—Point out *can't* on page 10. Explain that this is another way to say *cannot*.

## Post-Reading Activities

1. Ask students to name where each person in the family works.
2. Discuss what jobs students would like to have as adults. Let them draw pictures of themselves in their new careers.

## Extension Activities

1. Ask students to say thank you to someone who works.
2. Let small groups interview school employees who have jobs students want to know more about. Have groups share their interviews with classmates.
3. Provide items used by people in various careers, such as a stethoscope, briefcase, and safety goggles. Let students use the objects to role-play different jobs.

## Related Literature

- *Henry Works* by D. B. Johnson (Houghton Mifflin, 2004)
- *Tony's Hard Work Day* by Alan Arkin (Gibb Smith, 2002)
- *When Mommy and Daddy Go to Work* by Joanna Cole (HarperCollins, 2001)

## Translation Notes

In this story, the English names have been replaced with Spanish names. Explain that some English names have Spanish versions that are quite similar, while other names do not translate as easily. For example, the name *Anna* is pronounced similarly in both languages, but there is no exact English translation for the Spanish female name *Consuelo*, which means *consolation*. *Kate (Catalina)* could also be *Catharina*, and *Jim (Jaime)* could also be *James*.

Little Stories for Little Readers • CD-104200

# Can I Go, Too?

**Written by Susan M. Ketch**   **Illustrated by George Ling**

## My family is very busy. They all go to work.

**My dad goes to his job at the store.**

**Can I go, too, Dad?**

**My sister goes to her job at the hospital.**

**Can I go, too, Kate?**

**My brother goes to his job at the pizza place.**

**Can I go, too, Jim?**

## My mother goes to her job at the office.

## Can I go, too, Mom?

I can't go to their jobs, but I can go to my job.

My job is at school!

# ¿Puedo ir yo también?

**Escrito por Susan M. Ketch**　　**Ilustrado por George Ling**

**Mi familia está muy ocupada. Todos van a trabajar.**

## Mi papá va a su trabajo en la tienda.

## ¿Puedo ir yo también, Papá?

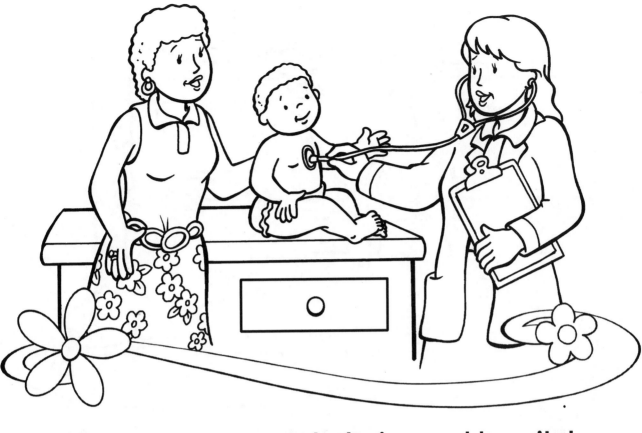

**Mi hermana va a su trabajo en el hospital.**

**¿Puedo ir yo también, Catalina?**

## Mi hermano va a su trabajo en la pizzería.

## ¿Puedo ir yo también, Jaime?

**Mi mamá va a su trabajo en la oficina.**

**¿Puedo ir yo también, Mamá?**

**Yo no puedo ir a sus trabajos, pero puedo ir a mi trabajo.**

**¡Mi trabajo está en la escuela!**

# The Sleepover
## Susie Gilbert      Level 6

**Number of English Words: 83**
**Number of Spanish Words: 84**

## Pre-Reading Activities

*Book Introduction:* The name of this book is *The Sleepover.* In this story, a girl describes fun things she did when she slept at school.

*Discussion Suggestions:* Ask, "What would you like to do at a school sleepover?" Explain the main focus of the sleepover is to spend extra time in the library so that their teacher can read to them, but the students get to do other things, as well.

*Picture Walk:* Have students compare the activities pictured to things students do when they are getting ready to go to bed at home.

*Word Work:*
Sight words—Students should learn to sight read the pronouns *I* and *we.*
Structure—Compare present and past tense of words. Point out the differences between *sleep/slept, wear/wore, sing/sang,* and *eat/ate.* Note similarities between *-ed* words.

## Post-Reading Activities

1. On a flannel board or bulletin board, help students "build" a school environment. Students can make small paper or fabric likenesses to place in the environment.
2. If your school does not have overnight "read-ins" like the one on which this story is based, hold a pretend sleepover for the class. Let students wear pajamas, dim the lights, and read stories.

## Extension Activities

1. Let students write or draw stories about what they would do if they could have a school sleepover. What would they do that they could not do during an ordinary school day? If they are writing, encourage them to use past tense.
2. Allow each student to draw a picture of himself at a sleepover, complete with pajamas and sleeping bag.

## Related Literature

- *Bearsie Bear and the Surprise Sleepover Party* by Bernard Waber (Houghton Mifflin, 2002)
- *Froggy's Sleepover* by Jonathan London (Viking, 2005)
- *Gorilla Sleepover* by Laura Driscoll (Disney, 2003)

## Translation Notes

*Patio* is a good example of a Spanish word that is used in English. It has the same meaning in both languages, unless it is combined with other words, as in the phrase *patio de recreo. Recreo* means *entertainment* or *recess.*

*Baloncesto,* the word for *basketball,* can also be *básquetbol.*

# The Sleepover

Written by Susie Gilbert

SCHOOL READ-IN TONIGHT! BRING YOUR SLEEPING BAGS AND PERMISSION SLIPS!

GREENWOOD ELEMENTARY

Illustrated by Stefano Giorgi

When we slept over at school one night . . .

. . . I wore pajamas and slippers.

I played basketball in the gym.

The cookies and milk in the cafeteria were good.

I liked the stories my teacher read in the library.

I sang silly songs and danced
in the music room.

I slept on a mat in the classroom with my
friends and my teacher.

The next morning, we ate bagels on the playground.

My teacher said that she needed to go home and take a nap.

# Quedarse
## A Dormir
### Escrito por Susie Gilbert

¡REUNIÓN DE LECTURA ESTA NOCHE! ¡TRAIGAN SUS SACOS DE DORMIR Y AUTORIZACIONES!

GREENWOOD ELEMENTARY

Ilustrado por
Stefano Giorgi

GREENWOOD ELEMENTARY

Cuando dormimos en la escuela una noche . . . .

**Me puse pijamas y zapatillas.**

**Jugué baloncesto en el gimnasio.**

**Las galletas y la leche de la cafetería estaban buenas.**

**Me gustaron las historias que mi maestra leyó en la biblioteca.**

Canté canciones tontas y bailé en la sala de música.

Dormí en una colchoneta en la clase con mis amigos y mi maestra.

**A la mañana siguiente comimos panecitos en el patio de recreo.**

**Mi maestra dijo que necesitaba ir a casa para tomar una siesta.**

# Whose Shoes?

Susan M. Ketch    Level 6

Number of English Words: 67
Number of Spanish Words: 87

## Pre-Reading Activities

*Book Introduction:* The name of this book is *Whose Shoes?* It is about different kinds of shoes that people wear for special activities.

*Discussion Suggestions:* Ask, "Do you wear different shoes when you do different activities, such as play shoes, shoes for dressing up, etc.? Why do people wear shoes? Why do we wear so many kinds of shoes?"

*Picture Walk:* As students look at each pair of shoes, let them predict the activity in the next illustration. Also, ask, "What do we call a person who dances?" Repeat for people who swim, run, and climb.

*Word Work:*
Sight vocabulary—Students should learn to read *the, whose, are,* and *and.*
Structure—Point out that *Whose shoes are _____?* and *¿De quién son los zapatos _____?* are recurring patterns.
Word analogies—Note similarities between *whose* and other question words. Examine the -'s chunk.
Vocabulary—Note color words and the words *sturdy, rock climber, dancer, swimmer, fluffy,* and *soft.* Help students give examples of each.

## Post-Reading Activities

1. Ask students if they can think of other kinds of shoes people wear when doing special activities. Do any students have shoes like those in the story?

2. Examine students' shoes to find different ways they are fastened to stay on students' feet.

## Extension Activities

1. Have each student trace the bottom of her shoe on paper, cut it out, and then compare its size to three classmates' shoe cutouts. Have students notice which are the largest and smallest shoes. Place all of the students' shoe cutouts on the wall in order from longest to shortest.
2. Place students' shoes in a pile and have students stand in a circle around it. On the count of three, each student should look for his shoes. Let the first student to find both shoes be the day's line leader.
3. On a sheet of paper, let each student draw a pair of shoes for a special activity.

## Related Literature

- *Boot Weather* by Judith Vigna (Albert Whitman, 1988)
- *Going for a Walk* by Beatrice Schenk de Regniers (HarperCollins, 1993)
- *Just Like Daddy* by Frank Asch (Aladdin, 1984)

## Translation Notes

*¿De quién?* literally means *of whom?*

*Colas* literally means *tail.* It is used here as the translation for *fin.*

# Whose Shoes?

Written by Susan M. Ketch    Illustrated by George Ling

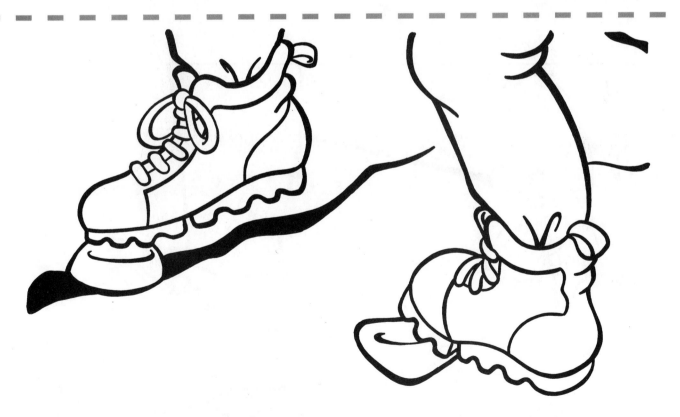

## Whose shoes are sturdy and brown?

**The rock climber's shoes are sturdy and brown.**

**Whose shoes are blue and white?**

# The runner's shoes are blue and white.

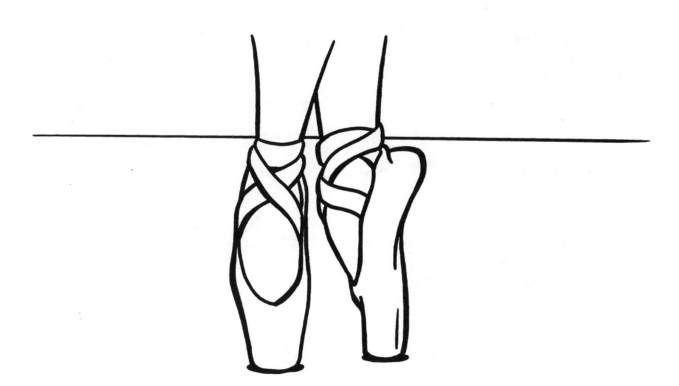

# Whose shoes are small and pink?

# The dancer's shoes are small and pink.

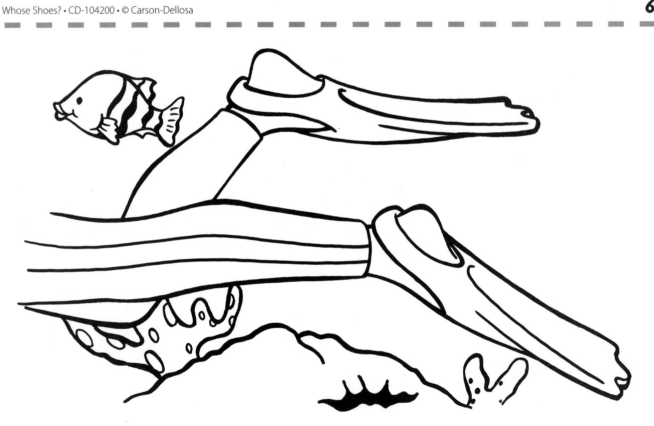

# Whose shoes are like fish fins?

# The swimmer's shoes are like fish fins.

Little Duck

DUCK

# Whose shoes are soft, fluffy, and yellow?

My shoes are soft, fluffy, and yellow.

¿De quién son los zapatos?

Los zapatos

Escrito por Susan M. Ketch          Illustrado por George Ling

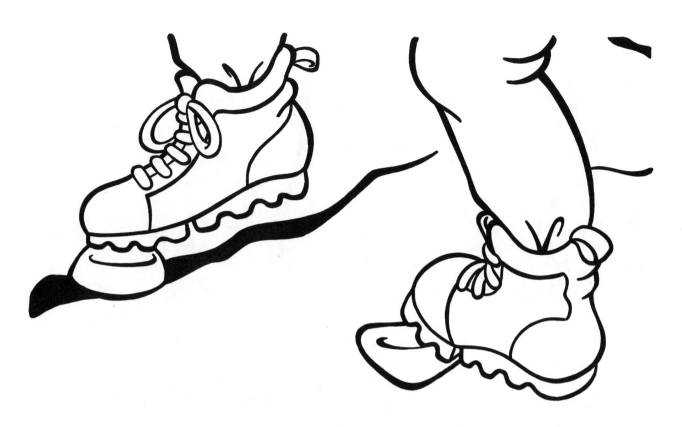

# ¿De quién son los zapatos fuertes y marrones?

# 1

# Los zapatos del escalador son fuertes y marrones.

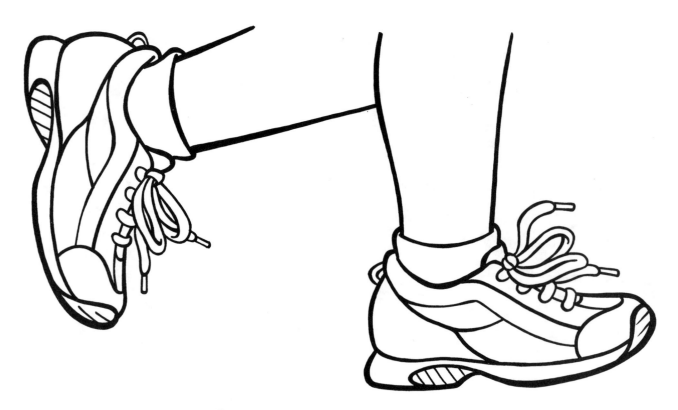

## ¿De quién son los zapatos azules y blancos?

## Los zapatos del corredor son azules y blancos.

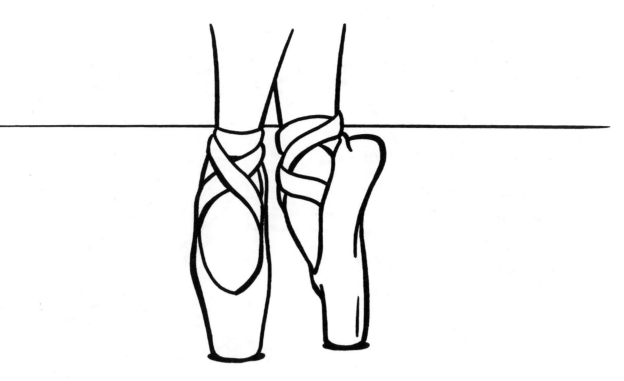

¿De quién son los zapatos pequeños y rosados?

Los zapatos de la bailarina son pequeños y rosados.

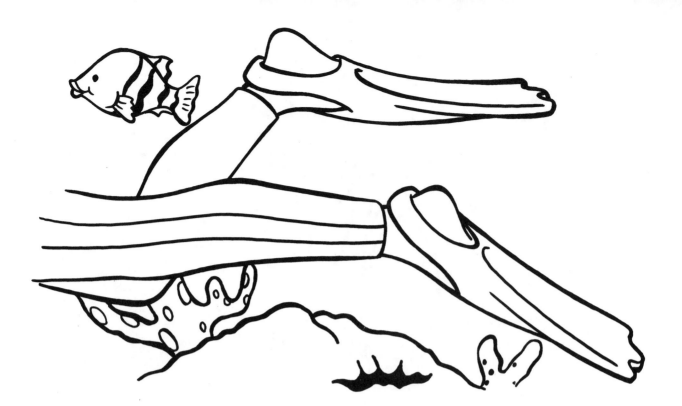

## ¿De quién son los zapatos comos las colas de un pez?

## Los zapatos del nadador son como las colas de un pez.

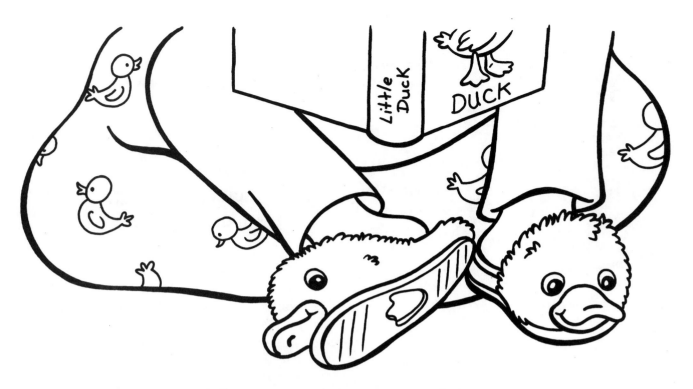

## ¿De quién son los zapatos suaves, acolchados y amarillos?

## Mis zapatos son suaves, acolchados y amarillos.

# Later, Sheri

Craig Johnson

Level 6

Number of English Words: 78
Number of Spanish Words: 85

## Pre-Reading Activities

*Book Introduction:* Mr. Stan wants Sheri to read and write, but she wants to do something else.

*Discussion Suggestions:* Ask, "Do you like to read and write? Are these easy or hard for you? What other things do you like to do?"

*Picture Walk:* Point out the classroom materials on each page. Ask students if they can tell what the class is doing. After reading, compare the clocks to the schedules on the title pages.

*Word Work:*
Sight vocabulary—Students should learn to sight read *can, we, do,* and *said.*
Punctuation—In English dialogue, quotation marks appear after the ending punctuation. In Spanish, quotation marks come before the ending punctuation. (Also see page 7.)
Structure—Point out that *Can we do something else?* and *Later, Sheri* are repeating patterns, as are *¿Podemos hacer otra cosa?* and *Después, Sheri.*
Word analogies—Compare the sounds in the words *can* and *Stan.*

## Post-Reading Activities

1. Discuss why Sheri wanted to do "something else." Ask what may have been the reason she wanted to read and write at the end of the story.

2. Point out that people usually like doing things they can do well. Have each student list things he can do well and have him teach one thing to a partner.
3. As a class, discuss whether it is important to do what the teacher says.

## Extension Activities

1. Note that Sheri is holding a classroom schedule on the title page. Let students make class schedules, either real or fantasy.
2. Have each student draw or write about a time when she learned something from a teacher. Was it something academic, like reading or writing, or something else?

## Related Literature

- *Lilly's Purple Plastic Purse* by Kevin Henkes (Greenwillow, 1996)
- *Notes from Mom* by Lynn Salem and Josie Stewart (Seedling, 1992)

## Translation Notes

In both languages, simple inflection can be used to change a statement into a question. An example of this is *¿Podemos hacer otra cosa?* Without the question marks, the sentence means *We can do something else.*

In Spanish, a person's title must be preceded by a definite article unless addressing that person. Thus, *El Sr. Stan dijo* should be used when talking *about* Mr. Stan, while *Sr. Stan* should be used when talking *to* him.

Reading 8:30-9:30
Writing 9:30-10:30
Social Studies 10:30-11:30
Lunch 11:30-12:00
Recess 12:00-12:30
Math 12:30-2:00
Science 2:00-3:00

**Written by Craig Johnson**
**Illustrated by Stefano Giorgi**

Mr. Stan said, "Let's read."
"Can we do something else?" asked Sheri.
Mr. Stan said, "Later, Sheri."

Mr. Stan said, "Let's write."
"Can we do something else?" asked Sheri.
Mr. Stan said, "Later, Sheri."

Mr. Stan said, "Let's read and write some more."
"Can we do something else?" asked Sheri.
Mr. Stan said, "Later, Sheri."

The next day, Mr. Stan asked Sheri, "Can we do something else?" Sheri said, "Later, Mr. Stan. I want to read and write!"

Después, Sheri

Lectura 8:30-9:30
Escritura 9:30-10:30
Ciencias Sociales 10:30-11:30
Almuerzo 11:30-12:00
Recreo 12:00-12:30
Matemáticas 12:30-2:00
Ciencia 2:00-3:00

**Escrito por Craig Johnson**
**Illustrado por Stefano Giorgi**

El Sr. Stan dijo, "Vamos a leer".
¿"Podemos hacer otra cosa"? preguntó Sheri.
El Sr. Stan dijo, "Después, Sheri".

El Sr. Stan dijo, "Vamos a escribir".
¿"Podemos hacer otra cosa"? preguntó Sheri.
El Sr. Stan dijo, "Después, Sheri".

El Sr. Stan dijo, "Vamos a leer y a escribir más".
¿"Podemos hacer otra cosa"? preguntó Sheri.
El Sr. Stan dijo, "Después, Sheri".

Al día siguiente, el Sr. Stan le preguntó a Sheri,
¿"Podemos hacer otra cosa"?
Sheri dijo, "Después, Sr. Stan. Yo quiero leer
y escribir".

# Our Puppies

Joy Gornto

## Level 6

Number of English Words: 57
Number of Spanish Words: 56

## Pre-Reading Activities

*Book Introduction:* This story is about two boys who are given two puppies by their mom and dad. The boys get to choose names for the puppies.

*Discussion Suggestions:* Ask, "Have you ever gotten to name a pet? What kinds of names can you think of for a cat, dog, bird, and fish? Why do these names fit the pets?" If you have a class pet, dicuss how its name was chosen.

*Picture Walk:* Draw students' attention to the size of the puppies in the basket. Ask students how long they think both puppies will fit in that basket.

*Word Work:*
Sight words—Students should learn to sight read *this, will, little, they,* and *said.*
Word analogies—Compare the sounds of the words *go* and *so,* as well as the beginning sounds of *this, they,* and *those.*

## Post-Reading Activities

1. If students have difficulty with the dogs' names, have them brainstorm other names that begin with the letter *n.* Remind them that if they substitute other names that begin with the letter *n,* it will not change the story's meaning.
2. Give students the magnetic letters *m, e, h, s, w,* and *b.* Ask them to make the word *me.* (Model this for the class.) Then, let students use the letters to make other short words that end with the letter *e,* such as *he, we, be,* and *she.* Expand the activity using the words *go* and *like* for models.

## Extension Activities

1. Let students draw pictures of pets they have or would like to have. Ask students to label the drawings with their pets' names.
2. Adopt a class pet or bring in a stuffed animal. Let students suggest names. Write the names on the board and let the class vote to choose the pet's name.

## Related Literature

- *Amos: The Story of an Old Dog and His Couch* by Susan Seligson (Joy Street Books, 1986)
- *Angus and the Ducks* by Marjorie Flack (Farrar, Straus and Giroux, 1997)
- *Please, Puppy, Please* by Spike Lee and Tonya Lewis Lee (Simon & Schuster, 2005)

## Translation Notes

*Cachorro* can also mean *cub* and is not the only word for *puppy. Perrito* (the word for dog, *perro,* combined with *-ito,* the diminutive suffix) is also common.

Little Stories for Little Readers • CD-104200

Mom and Dad gave us two puppies.

# Our Puppies

Written by Joy Gornto
Illustrated by Stefano Giorgi

"This puppy likes me," said Josh.
"This puppy likes me," said Zack.

They are so little that they fit in a basket.

"This puppy will be Nick," said Josh.
"This puppy will be Noel," said Zack.

Mom said, "What will you name
your puppies?"

# Nuestros cachorros

Escrito por Joy Gornto
Illustrado por Stefano Giorgi

"I like those names," said Mom.

# 2

Son tan pequeños que caben
en una canasta.

Mamá y Papá nos dieron
dos cachorros.

Mamá dijo, ¿"Cómo van a nombrar a sus cachorros"?

"Este cachorro me quiere", dijo Josh.
"Este cachorro me quiere", dijo Zack.

"Me gustan esos nombres",
dijo Mamá.

"Este va a ser Nicolás", dijo Josh.
"Este va a ser Noel", dijo Zack.

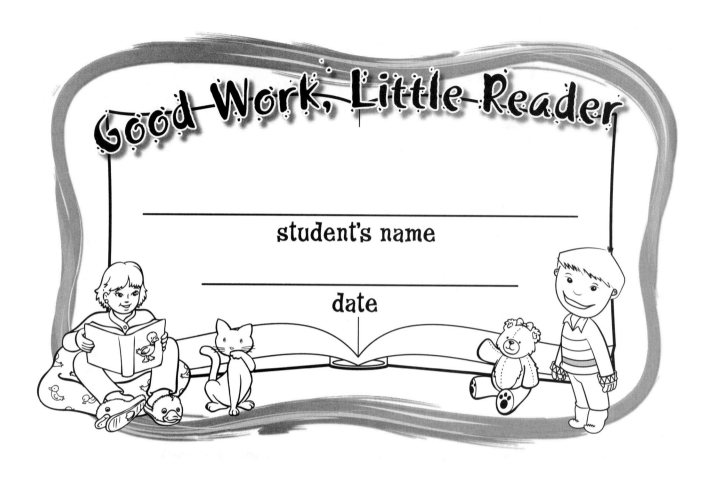

# Good Work, Little Reader

_____

student's name

_____

date

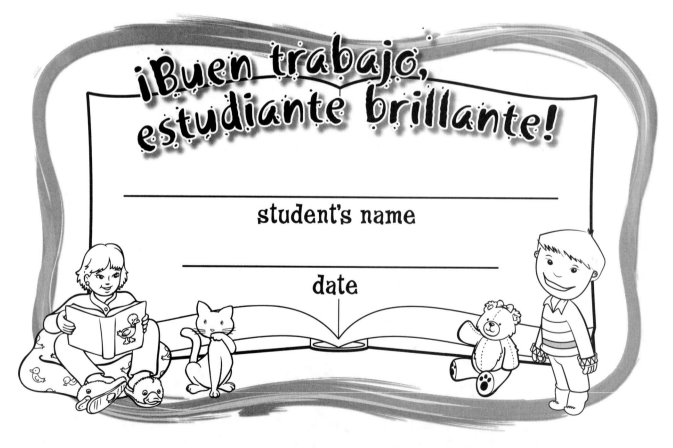

# ¡Buen trabajo, estudiante brillante!

_____

student's name

_____

date

Little Stories for Little Readers • CD-104200

# Making Your Own Books

The end of this book does not have to mean the end of your *Little Stories* experience. Let students create books of their own. Use the following ideas to help you expand the classroom library, help students increase the number of books in their homes, and continue to provide exposure to language arts activities.

- Laminate several pieces of paper, punch holes in them, and bind them with metal rings. Place the blank books in a center along with write-on/wipe-away markers. Every time you share literature with the class, place the book in a center. Let a few students at a time draw their own versions of the story on the reusable books. Encourage students to copy the words from the story, as well as draw pictures.
- Write parts of fairy tales, such as *The Three Little Pigs, Little Red Riding Hood,* and *Hansel and Gretel*, on pieces of paper. Leave the endings blank or leave blank pages in the middle. Let students write and draw the stories, filling in the blank pages with their own words and illustrations. Laminate the completed stories and either keep them in your classroom library or send them home with students.
- When a student writes a particularly good story, reward him by letting him share the story with the class. Photograph him as he reads and send the story and photos home to his family. Consider sending home a celebratory reading certificate, as well.
- Tell short stories about your students. On a piece of paper, write *This is the story of _____ _____*. Make a copy of this for each student and distribute it, along with blank paper, on the first day of school. Tell each student to write one question on each page. Explain that the questions should ask things they would like to know about a new friend. Then, pair students and have them ask each other the questions and illustrate the answers. Let each student present the book about her partner as a way of introducing him to the class.
- Document classroom and school events. When an event such as a field day, open house, class trip, or guest speaker occurs, let students draw stories about what happened. Have students bind their pages together. Date the books and place them in a plastic bin. At the end of the school year, let students read their books again to remind them of what happened during the year.
- Encourage other class bookmaking projects, such as class dictionaries, scrapbooks, study guides, alphabet books, and fact books.

# Spanish-English Glossary

**Teachers' Translation Notes:** Spanish words often change form according to tense, number, and gender. Therefore, what is correct vocabulary for one of these stories may not necessarily be correct in another context. Following are some examples of these situations.

Many Spanish adjectives change endings according to whether the nouns they modify are masculine or feminine and singular or plural. For example, the common word for *pink* is *rosado*, but the translation for *pink shoes* is *zapatos rosados*. For ease of use, the words in this glossary are translated exactly as students will see them in the stories. Remember that these words will be different in different sentences; teach common words as necessary.

Also, note that the Spanish verbs are listed exactly as they are conjugated in the stories. Therefore, if the different verb forms confuse English-speaking students, explain that just as English speakers use different verb forms with different pronouns (*I talk, he talks*), Spanish speakers do the same (*hablo, habla*). And, just as English verbs change form when their tenses change (*I talked*), Spanish verbs change, too (*hablé*). When teaching the Spanish verbs in isolation, concentrate on the infinitive forms.

## Title Pages:
**escrito por**  written by
**ilustrado por**  illustrated by

## That Made Me Mad! & ¡Eso me hizo enojar!:
**abrazo**  a hug
**amigo**  friend, buddy
**autobús**  bus
**el**  the
**en**  on
**enojar**  to be mad
**eso**  that
**lápiz**  pencil
**leche**  milk
**libros**  books
**los**  the
**me caí**  I fell
**me dió**  gave me
**me hizo**  made me
**me puso contento**  I became (or "got") happy
**mi**  my
**patio de recreo**  playground
**perdí**  I missed

**rompí**  I broke
**se me cayeron**  I dropped
**tiré**  I spilled
**un**  a

## Bubble Gum & Chicle
**a**  to
**ahora**  now
**casa**  house
**chicle**  gum
**cielo**  sky
**como**  as
**cuando**  when
**el**  the
**está creciendo**  it is growing
**grande**  big
**globo/globos**  bubble/bubbles
**hacer**  make
**hasta**  until
**a**  jugar
**me columpio**  I swing
**me gusta**  I like
**me hace**  it makes me
**mi**  my
**mientras**  while
**parece**  looks like
**pez**  fish
**puedo**  I can
**que**  that
**quiero**  I wish/I want
**ratón**  mouse
**salgo**  I go out
**tan**  as
**todo el día**  all day
**volar**  to fly (just "fly" in the story)
**un**  a/one (masculine)
**una**  a/one (feminine)

**124**

**The Party Place & El lugar de la fiesta:**
**adentro** inside
**amarillos** yellow
**azules** blue
**cómicos** funny
**de** of
**el** the
**en** in or at
**fiesta** party
**galletas** cookies
**globos** balloons
**jugo** juice
**la** the
**lugar** place
**¡Míranos!** Look at us!
**mucho** a lot
**muchos** many, lots, or more
**nos divertimos** we have fun
**para beber** to drink/for drinking
**regalos** presents/gifts
**rojos** red
**sombreros** hats
**son** they are
**tarta** cake
**tenemos** we have
**una** a (feminine singular)
**unas** some (feminine plural)
**ven** come
**verás** you will see
**verdes** green
**y** and

**My Best Buddy & Mi mejor amigo:**
**a** to
**a la pelota** with the ball
**a ti** to you
**amigo** friend, buddy
**bien** well
**bueno** good
**conmigo** with me
**dibujas** you draw
**él** he
**en lectura** in (at) reading
**eres** you are
**juegas** you play
**le digo** said to him

**lo que yo hago** that I do
**me abrazas** you hug me
**me dice** said to me
**mejor** best
**mi** my
**papá** dad
**sí** yes
**te gusta** you like
**todo** everything
**tú** you (familiar)
**yo** I

**The Builder & El constructor:**
**agujeros** holes
**al** combination of *a*, preposition meaning *on* and *el*, an article meaning *the*. Can also mean *to the* or *on the* (used here to say *the hammer hits the nail*)
**casa** house
**cinta de medir** tape measure
**clavo** nail
**constructor** builder
**cortará** will cut
**destornillador** screwdriver
**el** the (masculine singular)
**él** he
**hará** will make
**herramientas** tools
**la** the (feminine singular)
**las** the (feminine plural)
**le pegará** will hit
**los** the (masculine plural)
**madera** wood
**martillo** hammer
**medirá** will measure
**muchas** many
**para construír** to build (literally, use for building)
**pondrá** will put in
**sierra** saw
**taladro** drill
**tiene** has
**tornillos** screws
**una** a (feminine singular)
**usa** he uses

### As Big . . . & Tan grande como . . . :

**almohada** pillow
**cabeza** head
**como** as
**cuerpo** body
**es** is
**hermano** brother
**libro** book
**manos** hands
**mi** my (singular)
**mis** my (plural)
**pies** feet
**plato** plate
**rompecabezas** puzzle
**son** are
**soy** am
**tan grande** as big
**tan grandes** as big (plural)
**un** a (masculine)
**una** a (feminine)
**yo** I

### The Ocean & El océano:

**a los** to the (used with the reflexive verb comerse)
**agua** water
**alejarse** to escape from
**aloja** it houses
**arena** sand
**castillos** castles
**chicos** small
**comerse** to eat
**conchas** seashells
**corales** coral
**cuerpo** body
**de** of
**divertido** fun
**el** the (masculine singular)
**en** in
**enormes** big
**es** is
**está** it is
**excavar** to dig
**gran** big
**grande** big
**hacer** to make
**la** the (feminine)
**lleno** full
**los** the (plural)
**muchas** much or many

**océano** ocean
**olas** waves
**para** in order to
**para jugar** to play
**peces** fish
**pequeño** small
**pez** fish
**plantas** plants
**playa** beach
**que** that
**quiere** wants
**rocas** rocks
**se esconden** hide
**tiene** it has
**un** a
**un lugar** a place
**van** they go
**vienen** they come
**y** and

### Can I Go, Too? & ¿Puedo ir yo también?:

**a** to
**el** the (masculine)
**en** in
**escuela** school
**está** is
**familia** family
**hermana** sister
**hermano** brother
**hospital** hospital
**la** the (feminine singular)
**mamá** mother
**mi** my
**muy** very
**no puedo** I cannot
**ocupada** busy
**oficina** office
**papá** father
**pero** but
**pizzería** pizza shop
**su** your
**sus trabajos** their jobs/work
**tienda** store
**todos** everyone
**trabajar** work
**trabajo** work
**va** goes
**van** go

**126**

**The Sleepover & Quedarse a dormir:**
**a** to
**a la mañana** in the morning
**amigos** friends
**bailé** dance
**baloncesto** basketball
**biblioteca** library
**buenas** good
**cafetería** cafeteria
**canciones** songs
**canté** sang
**casa** home
**clase** class
**colchoneta** mat
**comimos** we ate
**con** with
**cuando** when
**de** of
**dijo** said
**dormí** I slept
**dormimos** we slept
**dormir** to sleep
**el** the (masculine singular)
**en** in
**escuela** school
**estaban** were
**galletas** the cookies
**gimnasio** gymnasium
**historias** stories
**ir** to go
**jugué** I played
**la** the (feminine singular)
**las** the (feminine plural)
**leche** milk
**leyó** read (past tense)
**maestra** teacher
**me gustaron** I liked
**me puse** I put on
**mi** my (singular)
**mis** my (plural)

**necesitaba** she needed
**noche** night
**panecitos** bagels (literally, small bread)
**para** to (used here like *in order to*)
**patio de recreo** playground
**pijamas** pajamas
**que** that
**quedarse a dormir** staying to sleep
**sala de música** music room
**siesta** nap
**siguiente** after
**tomar** to take
**tontas** silly
**una** a or one
**y** and
**zapatillas** slippers

**Whose Shoes? & ¿De quien son los zapatos?:**
**acolchados** fluffy
**amarillos** yellow
**azules** blue
**bailarina** ballerina
**blancos** white
**colas** fins
**como** like
**comos** like
**corredor** runner
**de** of
**¿de quién?** whose
**del** of the
**del + a noun = possessive** (for example, del corredor means the runner's)
**escalador** climber
**fuertes** strong
**la** the (feminine singular)
**las** the (feminine plural)
**los** the (masculine plural)
**marrones** brown
**mis** my
**nadador** swimmer
**pequeños** small
**pez** fish
**rosados** pink
**son** are
**suaves** soft
**un** a or one
**y** and
**zapatos** shoes

**Later, Sheri & Después, Sheri:**
**a** to
**al día** on the day
**algo** something
**cosa** thing
**después** later
**dijo** said
**El Sr.** Mr.
**escribir** to write
**hacer** do
**leer** to read
**más** else
**otra** other
**podemos** we can
**preguntó** asked
**quiero** I want
**siguiente** following
**vamos a** let's go
**y** and
**yo** I

**Our Puppies & Nuestros cachorros:**
**a** to
**a ser** to be
**caben** they fit
**cachorros** puppies
**canasta** basket
**cómo** what (in this context; can also mean how)
**dijo** said
**dos** two
**en** in
**esos** those
**este** this
**Mamá** Mama
**me gustan** I like
**me quiere** likes me
**nombrar** to name
**nombres** names
**nos dieron** gave us
**nuestros** our
**Papá** Papa
**pequeños** small
**que** that
**son** they are
**sus** your
**tan** so
**una** one
**va** go
**van a** you are going
**y** and

© Carson-Dellosa    Little Stories for Little Readers • CD-104200